AF506780

SYNOPSIS

"Amidst life's emotions, events, and everyday moments, wisdom quietly awaits. This collection of poetry and sayings, is my humble attempt to capture and share these unspoken lessons, inviting you to pause, reflect, and uncover the beauty hidden in the ordinary."

Life speaks to us in whispers through fleeting emotions, mundane moments, and the ebb and flow of daily events. Yet, amidst the rush, we often miss the quiet wisdom tucked within these experiences. This book is my humble offering to slow the world down for just a moment, inviting you to pause and notice what often goes unseen. In these pages, you'll find poems and sayings inspired by life's subtle lessons those that emerge from joy, sorrow, uncertainty, and stillness. This collection is not meant to prescribe answers but rather to provoke reflection. It's an invitation to engage with the ordinary and uncover the extraordinary that lies hidden within it.
Take a breath. Let each line meet you where you are, offering space to think, feel, and connect. You may find new perspectives, or perhaps rediscover things you've always known but forgot along the way.
May these words serve as gentle reminders that wisdom isn't something distant or rare it's woven into the fabric of every moment, waiting to be noticed.

I hope this book speak to you all.

Thank You

Before you step into the pages of this book, I want
to take a moment to say thank you.
Thank you for choosing to spend your time here,
exploring these poems and reflections. It means
more than words can express. Each thought shared
within these pages is a piece of my journey, and
now, it becomes part of yours.
Writing is only half the journey; the other half lies
in your reading, your reflections, and what these
words awaken in you. Whether they bring comfort,
inspire reflection, or simply offer a quiet moment, I
am grateful to walk alongside you in this shared
space.
This collection is as much yours as it is mine. Thank
you for opening your heart and mind to it. I hope
these pages resonate with you in ways that are
meaningful, however big or small.
With sincere gratitude,

SHANGTIBA RUDY

Welcome to the first volume of Gentle Whispers.
As we embark on this journey together, I invite
you to explore the themes and stories that weave
through these pages. This book is just the
beginning; there are two more volumes waiting to
unfold. The release of those future installments
will depend on the love and support this book will
receive. Your enthusiasm and feedback will guide
how quickly the next chapters come to life.
I genuinely welcome your thoughts, questions, or
simply a friendly hello. If you'd like to reach out,
you can contact me through the following:

Email: shangtibarudy@gmail.com
shangtiba_rudy

Thank you for allowing Gentle Whispers into your
life. I look forward to sharing this journey with
you and hearing what resonates with you along the
way.

Gentle Whispers Vol 1
The unspoken whispers

DAY 1 OF 365

ACKNOWLEDGEMENT

In this poem, my adaptation of "The Mask We Wear", draws inspiration from the profound work of Paul Laurence Dunbar, a distinguished African-American poet a poem called "We Wear the Mask". His exploration of societal masks offers timeless insights, which I honor with deep reverence for his enduring contribution to literature. Paul Laurence Dunbar's legacy continues to resonate, guiding my creative journey with his poetic brilliance.

- Thought:

I believe that this world is beautiful.
I also believe that with this beauty there is a flaw, judgments, where we need wear a mask, mask of being okay when you're not, that smile when you're broken inside, that laughter when you're packed with stress and worries, no one to pour on. But there's God whom we confess things, share things, pour everything without fearing of being judged, and he fixes things when the world couldn't.

The mask we wear.

I speak blessings towards the mask that guides to
night.
I speak joy and peace beneath the mask we hide.
Don't you think the world is overly wise,
The world be overly wise,
In counting our tears and sighs?
Don't they know that with bleeding hearts we
smile?
And wear the mask that grins and lies.

With every laugh, there's hidden tear,
As we portray joy while wrestling fear,
Behind the mask, emotions play,
In the shadows, they quietly stay.

A flower shattered, beyond repair.
"Restore," I whisper, but silence is my plea,
Like my doubts, remains in me.
But Oh, Great Christ! Those dreary cries, now
dies.
To thee from tortured soul arise.
From you my tortured soul arises.

No mask to feign. No mask to feign.
 Glory to Thee
 Glory to Thee.

DAY 2 OF 365

The words I have not spoken to avoid hurting their feelings have hurt me more by remaining unspoken.

DAY 3 OF 365

I am sorry for the
generation that try to find
healing and true love in
person.

DAY 4 OF 365

We all carry heavy heart in
deep silence.

This is the debt we pay to live.

DAY 5 OF 365

> **We can never rush our growth.**

If life takes to to hard journey remember that it's time for you to get stronger.
You know, we can't really rush our growth. It's like how a seed needs time to germinate, sprout, and eventually bloom. Our personal development unfolds at its own pace, too. Every experience we go through, every challenge we face, and those moments we take to reflect they all shape who we are.
When we try to hurry things along, we often end up with only superficial changes. But true growth? That happens in those quiet, sometimes uncomfortable moments. It's in those times of patience and persistence that we learn the most about ourselves.
So, if you're feeling stuck or frustrated, remember that it's all part of the process. Embrace where you are right now; every step you take is important. Trust that, with time, you'll blossom into the person you're meant to be. Keep going you're doing better than you realize.

DAY 6 OF 365

The things that gives you
butterflies will also give you
heart attack.

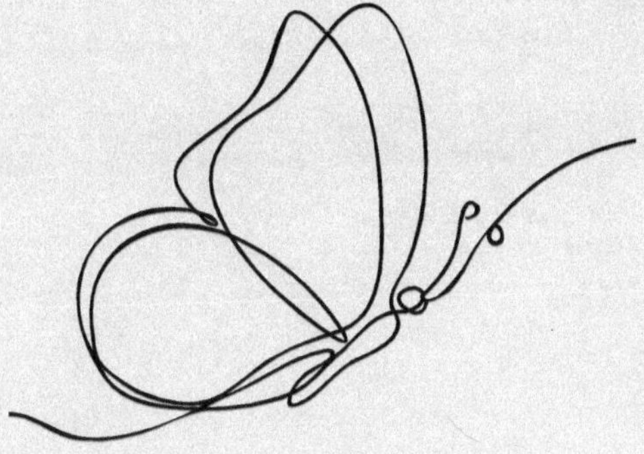

DAY 6 OF 365

DAY 7 OF 365

I removed the knife you
stab me, I bleed yet I stand
front and smile, I call it
forgiveness

DAY 8 OF 365

I was scattered like dry
leaves, and even when
someone gathered me, it
was only to burn.

We're prisoner of our own thoughts.

You know, we really are prisoners of our own thoughts sometimes. We get stuck replaying the same worries, doubts, or memories, and it can feel like we're trapped in a loop we just can't break. It's crazy how much power our own mind can have over us, isn't it?
But the thing is, those thoughts aren't the whole truth they're just stories we tell ourselves. The good news is, we have the ability to change the narrative. It's not easy, but the first step is recognizing when we're stuck and reminding ourselves that we don't have to believe every thought that comes up.
So, if your mind feels like a prison right now, just know you're not alone. Take it one breath, one thought at a time. You have the power to loosen the chains, even if it's little by little. And trust me, freedom starts with the smallest shift in perspective. Keep going you're stronger than you think.

DAY 10 OF 365

What right do I have to their good byes?
What excuses do I have to let them stay?
My soul has always been weak to hold someone
dear to me.

DAY 11 OF 365

Someone asked me what it means
to be lost. I told them, waiting
through every long night, for dawn.

DAY 12 OF 365

For a fleeting moment of
happiness, we've sacrifice
unimaginable joy and
gained countless regrets that
we can never undo.

DAY 13 OF 365

A heart doesn't have to stop to be dead.

A heart can break without a sound,
Alive, yet buried deep underground.
Beating softly, wrapped in despair,
Empty and aching in open air.

DAY 14 OF 365

The more we add sacrifices
and compromises, the more
we understand the meaning
of love in life.

DAY 15 OF 365

If you interpret my heart
you'd say I am suffering
from capital punishment.

DAY 16 OF 365

We all walk with the story
inside us, it is meant to be
told not to keep within'
ourselves.

DAY 17 OF 365

May be we're the unlucky
one who doesn't identify
bad people until and unless
we get betrayed.

DAY 18 OF 365

I am confident says my pride, I am bold
and happy says my life.

How long you gonna lie says my heart.

DAY 19 OF 365

My heart's full of gold for
the people i love.

DAY 20 OF 365

My delusion thinks he can
keep someone forever.

DAY 21 OF 365

Letting people to become
your home might turn you
to be homeless.

DAY 22 OF 365

The love that the world
bestowed upon me is
incomparable to the sublime
grace i have been endowed
with, by God.

DAY 23 OF 365

We don't have to hate forever
because of how it ended. The hate
will never let you to repair our
heart.

DAY 24 OF 365

I have been perceived as the
most awful and unworthy
person by others, yet in the
eyes of God i am neither.

DAY 25 OF 365

Forgiveness is always for
our mental peace.

Unburden.
Forgiveness, a quiet gift we give,
A gentle letting go, a way to live.
In the weight of grudges, we find no ease,
But in the act of forgiving, we find our peace.

With each release, the heart can mend,
A soothing balm, a chance to transcend.
For holding on tight only darkens the day,
While forgiveness lights up the path, showing the
way.

DAY 26 OF 365

We had people with our
words and lose them with
our actions.

DAY 27 OF 365

The true peace is freeing
yourself from attachments.

DAY 28 OF 365

Each of us journeys on the
last of healing from past.

DAY 29 OF 365

Bound by praise divided by rumour.

Today, we are bound by praise it lifts us, motivates us, and gives meaning to our efforts. Of course, it's needed; we all crave that validation to keep moving forward. But let not praise consume you, for the same hands that lift can just as easily let go. Praise weaves threads of belonging, but these bonds are delicate, easily frayed by whispers and doubt.
When rumours creep in, they unravel what seemed unbreakable, dividing us from those who once stood close. The line between admiration and isolation is thin what holds us today can undo us tomorrow. Perhaps the way forward is to accept praise without being bound by it, knowing that when rumours rise, they can tear through even the tightest ties.

DAY 30 OF 365

Surviving is not letting past
take too much of you.

DAY 31 OF 365

The art of noticing life has
always been missing from
me.

DAY 32 OF 365

My heart neither holds
grudge or revenge, what i
hold is pain.

DAY 33 OF 365

90 percent of the time my
words have been
misunderstood and 10th of
the time i have been
unheard.

DAY 34 OF 365

If i mention my scars you'd
not believe even if you did
believe you'd laugh at me.

Gentle Whispers vol.1

DAY 35 OF 365

There are different
standards of love some beg
out of love and i let it go.

DAY 36 OF 365

The difference between
someone with love and
someone without is that;
one grow wear, while other
is eager, only to grow tired
of love too.

DAY 37 OF 365

Even if i deny it for a
hundred of times, remind
me that i am not okay, if i
ever forget it'll cost me my
life, thinking i am fine.

DAY 38 OF 365

Perhaps my mother knew
me so well that when she
saw me laughing she asked,
why are you sad?

DAY 39 OF 365

It was a very strange food in
your memory, my entire life
almost passed by, having
food poisoned.

DAY 40 OF 365

I went to find peace and
ended up losing my sleep.

DAY 41 OF 365

Everyone is concerned
about how quite i am, while
i am consumed by the noise
raging inside my head.

DAY 42 OF 365

The way they accuse me was
like, I myself have given
testimony against myself.

DAY 43 OF 365

What right do we have to
complain about that the
people we love had not
loved us like before? people
even change God when
prayers are unheard.

DAY 44 OF 365

Which is greater, pride that
cost me the one I loved or
my humility that saved my
soul and those I love?

DAY 45 OF 365

If I would turn back time, I
would revisit every moment
I missed the chance to draw
closer to God.

DAY 46 OF 365

Someday I would like to see
my heart beating again.

DAY 47 OF 365

I have grown so old in my
heart that I now only seek
peace and silence.

DAY 48 OF 365

Most of us, before death has
kills us our loyalty did it
first.

DAY 49 OF 365

My heart is in war or else I
would find some words to
comfort your pain.

DAY 50 OF 365

The peak of my existence is
when I understood, loving
God and myself first is the
utmost priority.

DAY 51 OF 365

How strange is this love?
where some find heaven
others find hell.

DAY 52 OF 365

May your soul blossom for
the right person, for your
heart has endured many
breaks while blooming for
the wrong one.

DAY 53 OF 365

May all of us understand
that that at times with tears
and aching heart we had to
let go of things.

Hold is always painful.

DAY 54 OF 365

The more we learn about
people, the less we begin to
expect from them.

DAY 56 OF 365

You've enjoyed while I suffered, someone would
never be me, and someday somehow, if you try to
find a glimpse of me in others, remember that once
you had all of me but lose it all.

DAY 57 OF 365

Offer a knife to both your
enemy and your love ones;
it's the ones you love will
wound you first.

DAY 58 OF 365

If I let go of things that
bothers me I would be
forever alone.

DAY 58 OF 365

DAY 59 OF 365

Even when you said my
thoughts were all wrong,
still, you lingered in every
corner of my mind an ache I
couldn't silence, no matter
how I tried.

DAY 60 OF 365

In granting forgiveness, I
did justice to my soul, and
in that quiet mercy, he
found the peace his heart
had long sought.

DAY 61 OF 365

Our only true enemy is
overthinking. Rest of them
are passenger, just passing
by.

DAY 62 OF 365

I hope you love yourself
again, before you learn
hate, I hope you lean love.

DAY 63 OF 365

Do not let innocence blind
you, for your murderer will
always be someone you once
held dear.

DAY 64 OF 365

We keep prolong our
sorrows by searching for
happiness.

DAY 64 OF 365

DAY 65 OF 365

Caged my will.

They've washed my mind in lies
and told me to think freely,
cut the legs beneath me,
yet whispered run swiftly.

Chained my heart to their will,
yet asked me to dream.
Plunged me into the depths,
but wanted me to swim.

How can i breathe in a world
where they smother my cries,
and build walls around truth,
yet say, reach for the skies?

DAY 66 OF 365

But don't get soft on
somebody sweet talk, last
time it had almost killed me

DAY 67 OF 365

We are all healing from the
wounds that weren't our
fault.

DAY 68 OF 365

One can light up many hearts
with joy, yet still his heart
remains untouched by joy. I
am that one.

DAY 69 OF 365

So much still needs to be
written for this life;
we cannot afford to fade into
memory long gone or be
consumed by regrets already
ached in time.

DAY 70 OF 365

If you promised to stay, you'd
just be another name on the
list but if you actually stay,
you'd be the first person who
truly did.

DAY 71 OF 365

My body's acting alive when I
am not is the bravest thing I
have seen.

DAY 72 OF 365

I have buried countless emotions inside me; if I were to hug a flower, it would wither.

DAY 72 OF 365

DAY 73 OF 365

A part of us always suffer for
the emotions that remain
unburied

DAY 74 OF 365

Before the snowman song rings out once more, I
wish to donate my heart.

DAY 75 OF 365

Your presence always brought
healing and wounds together.

DAY 76 OF 365

Just because i have stop bleeding doesn't mean I
don't have scars. I laugh now even after those
helpless cries. I am warm today but that doesn't
erase the memory of my cold days. All of these has
made me strong, but I am afraid of what it will
take me to trust and love again.

DAY 76 OF 365

DAY 77 OF 365

If we start looking people from
our heart, They'd be no longer
beautiful.

DAY 78 OF 365

How can bed time be so
sorrowful when it meant to be
for rest.

DAY 79 OF 365

My silence was perfect
statement, meant for you to see
that I tried but you've never
understood, I stayed quiet
hoping you'd read all the
things that choked me to left
unspoken.

DAY 80 OF 365

My heart's an introvert, says
nothing though it feels
everything.

DAY 81 OF 365

We've loved someone for an
unhealthy amount of time to
the point where we become the
criminal of their sins.

DAY 81 OF 365

DAY 82 OF 365

I had a weak heart or else I
would fight to keep you for
little longer.

DAY 83 OF 365

How can I blame the thief
when I was the one who opened
the door.

DAY 84 OF 365

We all start with wanting too
much love and ended up
wanting too much peace.

DAY 84 OF 365

DAY 85 OF 365

When God has never written
for me, you've written my pain.

DAY 86 OF 365

Perhaps there's no place for me
to cry, but if I were fortunate
enough to shed tears, they'd
flood it.

DAY 87 OF 365

Everyone has their own share
of pain, some are writing, some
reading and the rest of us
feeling.

DAY 88 OF 365

Don't believe them; they come
just for a moment then left
scars to carry forever.

DAY 89 OF 365

May be we're that love that've
loved and never being told.

DAY 90 OF 365

Maybe there's reward in
heaven for being soft and kind
but in this world this has
choked me to death.

DAY 91 OF 365

When my brain refuses to
think, I bargain my heart to let
you in for the last time
everyday.

SHANGTIBA_RUDY

DAY 92 OF 365

Don't ask me why but I have
written this to let things live
when you weren't.

DAY 93 OF 365

How can it be that your
memories are more alive than I
am.

DAY 94 OF 365

We have break our hearts as if
we had a pair of extra heart,
just to keep someone.

DAY 95 OF 365

Unloving is not craving for
attention anymore.

DAY 96 OF 365

We all have loved people by
closing our hearts.

DAY 96 OF 365

DAY 96 OF 365

Why is happiness a preparation
to take something away?
Ever wondered, why sadness
comes after happiness?

DAY 97 OF 365

I hope we understand that we
must stop trying for someone
to become a green flag for you.
some are just meant to be a
lesson, stop trying.

DAY 98 OF 365

Love always doesn't comes
with blooming, it also comes
with withering.

DAY 99 OF 365

We're getting too comfortable
with the unreal forever and
promises of this world.

DAY 100 OF 365

That bullet, that pierced my
chest didn't hurt me as much as
seeing the face of the person
holding the gun when i turned
around.

DAY 101 OF 365

Sometimes for your mental
peace, let things be unheard
and unspoken.

DAY 102 OF 365

I have no control over fate or
else i would write your name in
every step i walk.

DAY 103 OF 365

We're losing everyday to win a
life.

DAY 104 OF 365

Some healing takes forever,
some names will always bleed
you.

DAY 105 OF 365

Some times we need to let go of
things with a smile that once
we cried and ask for.

DAY 106 OF 365

There's nothing left for my lips
to say, whatever it has to say
my tears have already told you.

DAY 107 OF 365

The night will always remind us,
how weak we are.

DAY 108 OF 365

I don't know about things but
regret punishment us all.

DAY 109 OF 365

"Some hearts are never bless to beat together."

While it can be painful to accept that not every connection lasts, remember that each one holds its own unique value. Every heart you encounter teaches you something about love, yourself, and the world around you. Embrace the lessons these experiences bring and carry them with you. They shape who you are and prepare you for the love that is meant for you—one that will resonate in harmony with your heart. Trust that even in the moments of separation, the journey of love continues. Your heart is resilient, and it will find its way to the connections that truly matter. Keep believing in love, for it has a way of surprising us when we least expect it.

DAY 110 OF 365

I hope one day you will regret the mess you have
made and the trouble you have caused me, but i
also hope you find peace and don't suffer over it.